Paul,

ENJOY!!

Tim

SPILLING
THE **BEANS**

What every entrepreneur needs
to know about Life Insurance

G. KIM HINKSON

Copyright © 2013 by G. Kim Hinkson

All rights reserved. No part of this book may be used or reproduced in any manner whatsoever without prior written consent of the publisher except in the case of brief quotations embodied in critical articles and reviews.

ISBN hardcover: 978-1-939758-26-2
ISBN eBook: 978-1-939758-35-4

ACKNOWLEDGMENTS

Special thanks to my loving wife, Kathy, and my brilliant children, Josh and Jessica, all of whom inspire me. I also want to thank my amazing team at Ocean West Financial Group whose efforts and talents have helped make not only our company successful, but this book as well. And of course, I would like to personally thank the amazing clients, such as yourself, who honour my team and me by telling us their stories and trusting us with their business.

FOREWORD

EVERY ONCE IN a long while, an opportunity comes along to peer behind the curtain. A chance is offered to look beyond the veil of complexity, confusion, and jargon to understand the mechanics of a thing: what it is, how it really works, and what the stakes are. These are rare glimpses given by experts who've gone rogue—outing their industry and granting the rest of us insider access. Kim Hinkson has created just that sort of opportunity with *Spilling the Beans*, an insider look into the world of large-policy life insurance.

I'll admit, when Kim first told me about the book, I was skeptical. We were having dinner in Chicago and getting to know each other for the first time. To take on the topic of insurance and make it relevant, to make it exciting, and to make it accessible to entrepreneurs, of all people, is a tall order. And then to top it off, Kim wasn't offering to dumb it down; he intended to expose how it really works from the

FOREWORD

inside. I was skeptical, as I said. But then, I'd only just begun to know him.

How wrong I was.

My experience with leaders of Kim's caliber in the advanced market of insurance comes from my work as the founder and president of The Wisdom Link, a leading intellectual capital development firm. My perspectives, good, bad or what have you, were honed over a decade by absorbing those of several hundred of the industry's top one-fourth of 1 percent of income earners, mavericks, and innovators. The unorthodox perspective of people like Kim has informed my own worldview and the manner in which I serve.

And from what I can tell, advisors like Kim are in short supply.

As I see it, the next generation of advisors are typically coming up without the sort of deep technical know-how or business acumen today's business environment requires. And from what I see, these downgrades in the industry training and technical expertise are degrading the quality of strategy and solutions. This cocktail of commoditization isn't only toxic to insurance advisors, it also heralds the eventual end to many of the most attractive business advantages for leveraging insurance. It is up to the veterans of insurance to lead now. It is up to the established advisors to make a shift from thinking like outlier producers to thinking like industry spokespeople, leaders, and transformers. That's the

FOREWORD

opportunity and the need; but it's not a call that many hear.

So over that first dinner in Chicago, my conversation with Kim ranged from the mundane to the spectacular, from opera to business to raising kids. If you haven't yet met Kim, you'd enjoy his sharp wit and the pleasure he takes in exchanging ideas. He's funny, eclectic, curious, and erudite. He's both a charmer and a straight shooter. I learned very quickly that he's an intellectual in a salesman's industry and his distinctions, those that set him apart from the rank and file, only begin there. The son of a wealthy and prominent businessman, Kim has the bearing of old-world landed gentry, the pragmatism of a world-class businessman, and the irreverent nonconformity of a retired rock star. He's wry, fashionable, and holds himself out like a sixteenth-century plantation owner on holiday at Lollapalooza. He's also rather fun to tease. He's the last thing you'd expect from an insurance man, and in many ways, I think that's been the secret to his success.

By the time the entrées were served, he'd begun to really tell me about the book. The more he spoke, the more buoyant and animated he became. He paid little attention to his meal while he shared the title and the goal: to demystify an industry that has long held her secrets close to the apron. Kim explained that he felt this book was a long time coming and much needed in today's business world. He shared with me the necessity and utility of life insurance in the

FOREWORD

succession-planning process, the time-sensitive opportunities afforded business owners through insurance, and how critical understanding and action are today due to shifts in legislation and regulation. And finally, he explained about his personal entrepreneurial roots and the passion he has to serve others.

And now, with *Spilling the Beans*, he is going to do all of that for you. Take it from me and count yourself lucky. Actually, don't take it from me. Read the book and decide for yourself.

Spilling the Beans takes the reader through the inside world of the insurance industry seen from the perspective of an advanced advisor and his clients. Unlike other books that teach the details of product, Kim's book explains how the machine works. He explains why top entrepreneurs invest in it, how the process works, what the insurance companies do to protect themselves, and finally, what to do to game the system to your firm's advantage. *Spilling the Beans* is a timely read and despite my initial suspicions, Kim has made the subject surprisingly interesting, relevant, and digestible.

Like other books before it that have cast a light of truth on a dimly lit subject matter, *Spilling the Beans* confronts an industry in upheaval and provides clear, direct advice at a time when it's most needed. And Kim, for all his brio and insight, is the most entertaining of guides. He is direct, concise, and unapologetic in his agenda: to arm the entrepreneurs

FOREWORD

of today for the battles ahead. He is a rare find; a masterfully skilled advisor with a big enough vision for service to extend his scope beyond his own business goals, his own locale, his own industry. Before dessert, I could tell I'd met the right man for the job at just the right time in the arc of his career.

So thank you, Kim. In every time of transition, there is great uncertainty and confusion. Some people step forward to lead and some retreat. Some hear the call and others deny it or never hear it in the first place. For business owners in today's uncertain world, Kim Hinkson is a leader who has stepped forward with a message whose time has come.

       Jon LoDuca
       Founder and President,
       The Wisdom Link

       Chicago, IL
       November 3, 2013

SPILLING THE BEANS

What every entrepreneur needs
to know about Life Insurance

IF YOU HAVE read the foreword to this book, you know a little bit about where I am coming from as a specialist in the Canadian large-policy life insurance industry that caters to very-high-net-worth individuals. The people I work for—who are people probably not unlike yourself—are busy movers and shakers at the top of their respective industries. They need the protection and liquidity that life insurance affords, but they do not have the time or know-how to get through the process. My entire business, Ocean West Financial Group, is geared towards efficiently and effectively helping these individuals attain the insurance they need to protect, preserve, and build their estates through life-insurance investment vehicles.

What I have learned in my years running Ocean West Financial Group is that my clients are often unaware of how complex and fraught the life insurance market can be. This is why I am writing this book, to really *spill the beans*, if you will, on this industry. I wanted to have a concise but informative text I could hand to the entrepreneurs that make up my clientele and say, "This is what you need to know. Here are the basics."

I understand the needs of entrepreneurs—they have surrounded me for the entirety of my life. My father owned several hotels, a business that had been in our family for three generations. It was clear from day one that his entrepreneurial spirit had rubbed off on me. The desire to always be selling something consumed me from a young age. Growing up, I sold lemonade from a stand and soon broke out into more innovative and less-crowded markets, selling light bulbs for the Boy Scouts of Canada and other items. I was also always selling myself, which I realized at a young age was my greatest asset. My first customers were my family, my grandparents and parents, and others, to whom I tried to prove my worth by taking on responsibilities and helping to solve problems whenever possible. As a young man, I started working at my father's first hotel, starting out as a desk clerk and working my way up to food and beverage manager, and I later rejoined him as an operations manager at a larger, more prestigious hotel in Regina, Saskatchewan.

In 1987, I was faced with a choice. We lost the hotel because it went into receivership due to unfortunate economic conditions. This left me having to decide what to do and where to go. Though Regina held a special place in my heart, it was important to me to always be moving onto bigger and better things, and that meant going to a bigger market—either Vancouver or Toronto. Vancouver made more sense because of the lifestyle it afforded my young family at the time. Originally, I had planned to go back into real estate, but was soon drawn to the financial services industry where I saw a largely unfilled need. My old entrepreneurial spirit had kicked in.

What was that need? While working in the family business, I had worked with our CPA who had put in place a family trust and did an estate freeze to protect our assets when we lost the business. He had us partially protected, but we were missing one key component of protection: life insurance. So I was after my father to buy life insurance to support the need within the estate, but he was resistant. As the only child in the business and the one with the most to lose if something happened to my father and we didn't have insurance in place, I could best see our exposure. There was no liquidity to pay for the capital gains tax in the business without considering conventional onerous options such as a bank loan, selling the hotel, and/or diverting cash flow from operations of the hotel. So we were stuck with these conventional options, which are more expensive than any form of life insurance. This meant that the estate would have to come up with the cash to pay for the taxes upon his passing, which would have been a hardship and would have come out of my pocket, as I was the last surviving shareholder upon my parents' passing.

That was when I recognized the huge and largely unmet need for entrepreneurs to have in place a life insurance policy that protects the exposure of their entire estate. (Estate preservation is the main need of the high-net-worth individuals that comprise my clientele today,) but the more I dug into the insurance market, the more I discovered that life insurance can be used for both succession planning and also as a means to effectively defer and eliminate tax burdens.

This was very valuable knowledge and I wanted to offer it to other business owners. As an entrepreneur and the former heir to a family business, I understood both the importance of estate tax planning and the need for comprehensive life insurance to complement and support tax planning and fully protect an estate. This is why I started my own business, Ocean West Financial Group, focusing on helping entrepreneurs make strategic and financially sound decisions about life insurance and succession planning. Having worked with consultants at my father's business, I understood the importance of harnessing outside expertise, and by making myself an expert in advanced life-insurance strategies, I would be able to offer something of real value to other business owners.

Why life insurance? The same reason anyone starts any business: because there was an unfilled need in the market.

I understood that insurance is the best way for entrepreneurs to protect themselves, their businesses, and their other interests. Many entrepreneurs are hyper-focused on their businesses—on the day to day, the current quarter—and while they may think long-term when making current business decisions, they often fail to recognize gaps in their exposure to risk.

The thing about life insurance is that it is only as good as it is comprehensive. I saw a need for entrepreneurs, especially high-net-worth individuals, to close gaps that expose them to risk. Life insurance policies are especially important to entrepreneurs with partners, which is the norm of course, because any buy–sell agreements need to be backed with enough insurance to ensure that, if one partner passes, there is enough liquidity to cover the entire buyout at the critical moment when the funds are needed. You cannot really count on any buy–sell agreement that is not fully insured for the fair market value of the business and its full rate of growth over a three- to five-year horizon.

Most entrepreneurs have their money tied up in hard assets like real estate, which can cause a liquidity issue in the case of an emergency. The company needs sufficient capital to keep operations funded and to allow the remaining partners to fully buy out the company without having to bring on the spouse of a deceased partner as a new partner, which should be avoided as the spouse rarely knows the business. It is far preferable in most cases for remaining partners to buy out the company and for the family to get money—but this can require a massive amount of liquidity.

This sort of liquidity can only be counted on if it is insured. So the instant liquidity afforded by a large and comprehensive life insurance policy also helps protect the family of the deceased and ensure that their financial needs are met and that they receive a fair compensation for their stake in the business without having to be made major shareholders.

So there are really two needs being met here by having sufficient liquidity that only life insurance can ensure: 1) protection for the family and 2) protection of the company and remaining partners via a fully insured buy–sell agreement to seamlessly transfer the deceased partner's share in the company to the remaining partners.

These sorts of cases are as common as they are complex. The need for a sound, effective, and flexible succession plan is the number one problem that entrepreneurs, their families, and their partners don't know they have. Few entrepreneurs have developed and managed a proper succession plan. I started Ocean West Financial Group (OWFG) because it became apparent to me that successful entrepreneurs like yourself need someone that understands the complicated world of life insurance. Very few financial advisors out there even work with policies of this size, and those that do often don't have the unique knowledge of the advanced insurance strategies that OWFG brings to the table.

SPILLING THE BEANS

As an entrepreneur, I identify with entrepreneurs and understand their needs. I know they are busy and that their time is best spent on their own businesses, not planning their taxes or estate. This does not mean that these things are not important—they are vitally so—but it does mean that you want to have a specialist on your side. You probably already have financial advisors, but these people do not do what we do, and they probably do not have the expertise in what is a niche area of financial planning. I am not a financial advisor, but we do work with your financial advisors in order to broker the best possible deal on life insurance and succession planning for you. We are advanced insurance specialists.

What does this mean? It means that we don't sell life insurance. We are *not* financial advisors. We are entrepreneurs and strategists.

As strategists, we work with a successful time-proven process based around the client's vision. The first step in our process when working with clients is the Vision Conversation, in which we help the clients define their vision of how things should be. We want to understand how they want their personal and professional affairs to look and be handled upon their passing. We consider our clients' family needs, business needs, risk tolerance, quality of life, corporate and personal financial needs, and other factors to bring our clients a well-designed, custom-tailored set of options that best suit their needs. This is what we mean by "strategic."

Our unique seven-step process—The Smart Strategies Program®—starts with an exploration of your vision and ends in successful implementation of no-gaps insurance and a succession plan that meets all of your personal and professional needs.

It is this process that makes us unique, efficient, reliable, and highly effective at meeting our clients' needs. The process is optimized for a level of efficiency that involves the client and their advisors no more than is necessary. Our process allows us to solve perplexing problems that you may not even know you have—namely, gaps in exposure to risk—in a strategic and streamlined manner. We realize how busy you are as a successful entrepreneur, and involve you as little as possible. The entire process is streamlined and balanced to be both highly efficient and effective.

We work with advisors, insurance companies, and multiple professionals in many fields in order to come up with a strategy that allows you to get the best life insurance at the lowest possible price. This means, if all goes well, a comprehensive life insurance that covers all of your personal and business needs at <u>no net</u> cost to you. This may sound too good to be true, but I promise you it is not. We utilize cost-effective tax advantages in order to create insurance policies that, while not free, relieve your tax burden in an amount roughly proportional to the cost of the policy. (More on this later.)

Why a strategist in addition to an advisor? Because your financial advisors are focused on only one thing—finance. We coordinate your inner circle of trusted advisors, such as lawyers, accountants, as well as our own specialists. We have a pool of talent we draw upon while moving you through the process so that we can deal with any problems that arise while implementing the creation of your succession plan. Do realize that problems can and most likely will arise: these strategies require advanced specialist knowledge, and a misstep can result in a denial of full coverage, especially for extremely-high-net-worth individuals. You really need a skilled and knowledgeable strategist leading the way. You want someone coaching and quarterbacking the process for you.

And that's where we come in. The life insurance industry has the tendency to make already-complex information more complex—so complex that even the brilliant, but busy, entrepreneurial clients with whom we work struggle to fully understand the market. They don't have the specialist knowledge. Why would they? It's not their business.

But it is mine. And it's my life. Upon initial consultation, we find that most of our clients at Ocean West Financial Group have hidden needs that they didn't fully understand or appreciate. They are often unaware of their own exposure and missed opportunities to reap the rewards of tax-advantaged insurance strategies. What these people, and perhaps you are one of them, need is someone with the insider knowledge of the complex world of large-policy life insurance for entrepreneurs.

That's where this book comes in.

I am writing this book for the same reason I started Ocean West Financial Group all of those years ago: because I wanted to really spill the beans on the life insurance industry. This is a no-nonsense look at the things successful entrepreneurs must understand about life insurance. You or your business partners may have exposure you do not realize. You may have financial and tax-relief opportunities you are missing out on—opportunities that are soon to disappear forever.

Life Insurance Is a Luxury Product

I GET IT. Life insurance is not something that usually captures the imagination. Let's face it: most people don't get really fired up over life insurance.

Not, that is, until they really need it.

That's the thing about insurance though: we undervalue the protection it provides because, while we see money going out in premiums every month, we forget about the protection a policy affords, because we do not need the liquidity that life-insurance proceeds afford until, well, until our estate and family really need them. As such, we tend to view insurance as an afterthought, but you do so at your own detriment. Life insurance is essential in protecting our assets, families, and business interests when we pass.

Life insurance may not be as sexy as a new Ferrari or BMW or as flashy as diamond jewelry, but that does not mean it is not just as much of a luxury item. Actually, these larger policies that we work with are far more exclusive than the ownership of any luxury car or fancy bauble. The products we work with effectively act as guaranteed liquidity up to around $130 million. Where else can you create over a $100 million of wealth out of thin air?

Products such as these are exclusive to the most privileged and elite individuals in the developed world. Others do not have access to them. They don't even have a need for them. It is only individuals with a net worth, either in assets or stakes in their company, that are truly worth tens or hundreds of millions of dollars who can even make use of such a luxury item.

Furthermore, you will see a real, measurable benefit *during your lifetime* when you employ the advanced insurance strategies we use. For one, you and your business will be protected in the event of a business partner passing. But the life insurance proceeds aren't the only benefit. You will actually save money by using our strategies and the tax-advantaged products we utilize, and you will see these savings *during your lifetime*. The net effect of this is typically a neutral, and sometimes even positive, cash flow.

The truth is that life insurance is neither as simple nor as ubiquitous as you might believe. Today, life insurance is only available in advanced nations that are both affluent and also politically stable. And not everyone fortunate enough to live in such nations, such as Canada, are able to afford or access quality life insurance that works for them. I am currently working with a client who travels regularly to the Middle East for business and keeps a residence there in a region that is often a hot spot of political strife and terrorist activity. Today he is able to get life insurance there, but if something happens there today, before he makes it through the underwriting process and his policy is in place, any major disruption, such as an event of terrorism or political strife, could result in a denial of coverage. We are working with him to get him through the process as quickly as possible.

Quality life insurance policies are even beginning to disappear for those who reside in the wealthy, developed world because of changes in the world market and increased regulation. The best tax-advantaged insurance strategies that are available now are currently under attack. The Canadian government is trying to do away with these strategies in order to extract more in taxes and return market risk to the industry. Large life insurance policies that utilize accounts where the rate of returns on a tax-exempt account is linked in any way to the loan rate are being phased out because the government has deemed them unfair.

Thankfully, the government is making concessions and is grandfathering some existing programs that are currently in place before changes to the law. They have made it clear to the industry that things will change but that they will have the back of current policyholders—so you can reasonably expect to be grandfathered in under the old laws if your policy is in place before any changes. Anyone who has grandfathered strategies can consider themselves part of a private club: once your policy is in place, you have the comfort of knowing grandfathering will prevail, and you will be one of few people who likely took advantage of it.

Everyone else is out of luck. Everyone else will have to make do with what can still be had. But there is still time.

The recent changes to the 2013 Canadian budget close off some of our strategies and have forced us to seek out new compliant strategies. We actually have more viable options at our disposable now, but changes are always happening and the government is continuing to close loopholes.

Life insurance is important for everyone, but it is exceedingly important for entrepreneurs with their own successful business. For the kind of high-net-worth individuals I work with at Ocean West Financial Group, life insurance is the best tool for protecting their business and preserving their estate through succession planning. Founders, CEOs, owners—these individuals are assets to their company, and they need to be insured. They are worth millions of dollars to their businesses. Their stakes in their businesses are literally priced at millions or billions of dollars of worth. Most such individuals will have partners with whom they must have a solid buy–sell agreement in order to keep the business intact should one partner pass away. An uninsured buy–sell agreement is not worth the paper it is printed on if the liquid funds aren't there for the buying partner to purchase the seller's stake at the critical moment of buyout of the shares. This is one example showing why life insurance becomes a necessity.

In these cases, life insurance becomes more than just insurance. It becomes an important component of legacy planning, financial management, and responsible and sound business practice. This is the reason that the entrepreneurs we work with take out such large policies, in the millions and tens of millions of dollars. The protection that life insurance provides is thus valuable, albeit a luxury item, and an absolute necessity in the current business climate.

So you see now that life insurance is becoming increasingly rare. As such, you should value a quality life-insurance strategy as the luxury item that it is and move to acquire coverage while the best, most tax-advantageous plans are still available to you.

MARK TO MARKET rules would allow insurance Proceeds to be included in Estate Value Today as is with annuity!

G. KIM HINKSON

If You Are Paying $1 for Life Insurance, You Are Paying Too Much

MAYBE YOU ALREADY have a basic life insurance policy. This is not the kind of policy we are talking about. The clients we deal with acquire life insurance policies for tens of millions of dollars, and on occasion, over a hundred million dollars. These large policies are needed to cover the worth of a high-net-worth individual's stake in their company and estate so that when they pass away, their family and estate are protected as well as their business partners' stake in the business. These amounts allow the remaining partners, as we have said, to be sure that the liquidity is in place to buy out policyholder's stake in the company. This way the family gets cash, the estate is preserved, and the company can continue operations without having to take on a new majority shareholder or partner in the spouse. Typically, it is ideal if all partners and majority shareholders in a company are fully insured so that everyone has peace of mind.

As with a smaller life insurance policy, these larger policies include a premium, often a substantial one commensurate with the size of the policy. So why then do we say that it can cost you nothing?

This is where our *advanced insurance strategies* come in. Without getting too technical, the basic idea is that these extremely large life insurance policies allow you to take advantage of tax-advantaged plans. The plans are associated with large investment accounts. For purposes of calculating your income taxes, life insurance policies come in two flavors: exempt and non-exempt policies. We only use exempt plans, which afford clients the benefit of tax sheltering on the growth of investments within the policy, especially when compared to traditional investments. Furthermore, the death benefit proceeds (including the cash value of the policy, not just the investment earnings) are paid out tax-free upon the death of the policyholder, making these policies ideal for succession planning. The investment accounts associated with these policies are a good place for the wealth of an estate to be stored and transferred without being subject to taxation.

Another benefit of these policies is that when you employ our strategies, you are able to avoid tying up your cash flow in paying premiums, because you will be able to receive a proportionally sized reduction in income taxes. In this way, you can circle the maximum amount of your personal cash flow back into your own business for reinvestment. Why tie up money in a policy when you can put your money back into the business that you control directly? That's where you are going to make your best returns, not in an investment account. At Ocean West Financial Group, we recognize that you do the best job of managing your money, much better than anyone else, and that is a philosophy we have built our strategies around.

The other benefit of using an advanced insurance specialist like us is that we have the time and expertise to be strategic about your succession plan. Just like you know how to make best use of your money, you also know how to make best use of your time. The most strategic use of your time as a successful entrepreneur with your own business is to spend your time working on that business, not on trying to decode the complex world of larger-policy life insurance.

Our clients will earn a far better return on their time tending to their businesses than they can trying to negotiate a life-insurance contract. The strategic move is to leave that to a specialist like us.

SPILLING THE BEANS

Life Insurance Is a Scarcity

SO AS YOU can see, there is no question as to the value of life insurance. But what you may not yet realize is its *mounting* value due to increasing scarcity. This is an ongoing process as access to life insurance continues to diminish over time. This is why I wrote this book: to let you know that the best opportunities to obtain quality larger-policy life insurance and affordable succession planning are going away. They are being phased out by the government, the industry, and the economic climate.

There are several reasons for the shift in life-insurance access. Among the biggest and most apparent factors are the changes to government regulation that govern the industry. The Canadian government has begun to deem "unfair" some of the strategies that utilize policies that link the loan rate with the internal rate of return of the cash value in the exempt account—they don't want guarantees on the investment because the government wants to encourage market risk. What this means for the consumer is that many of the best options available now will soon be gone forever unless you get a policy grandfathered in before the changes. As I said, these changes have already begun, beginning with changes made in the 2013 Canadian budget, and we fully expect further changes. They are on the way. How do we know? Because the government has clearly announced their intentions!

Another factor contributing to increased scarcity of life insurance is our current, and probably permanent, low-interest-rate environment. Low interest rates are bad for insurers because they make it harder for insurance companies to make a profit from their two main products: life insurance and annuities. Both of these products require long-term returns on investments, which are hampered by low interest rates. Traditionally, insurers would sell policies and use the proceeds from premiums to invest in government bonds that yielded a 6 percent or more return. With interest rates so low, these same investments struggle to even keep up with inflation. As a result, insurance companies are experiencing historically low margins and low profits.

Of course, such losses are passed onto the policyholder where possible; when not possible, which is the case when a policyholder is deemed too expensive or risky to insure given the new regulations and the current economic climate, the insurer backs out of that segment of the market. This is cutting more and more marginally insurable candidates out of the market for life insurance. In this way, low interest rates are making comprehensive and affordable coverage exceedingly difficult to attain and more expensive to acquire. We have seen rates increase an average of three times every year for the last two years, and you can expect this trend to continue.

Another factor contributing to the mounting scarcity of life insurance in Canada is trends in demographics.

Proportionately, Canada has just as many baby boomers as the United States does. These baby boomers are now reaching retirement age in greater numbers each year, and the life insurance industry finds itself in a curious situation: as a nation, Canada has more and more people in need of life insurance combined with a paradoxical shrinkage in the availability of life insurance.

This imbalance creates a supply-and-demand issue, shifting the industry from a buyer's market to a seller's market. This creates obvious challenges for the consumer, and it is not just a matter of costs, though it is driving costs up. This dynamic has significantly impacted the process by which Canadian life insurance companies handle underwriting—the process by which insurance companies determine whether you are eligible for their insurance products and services. In short: there are fewer people in the market and they have fewer options available to them. And as boomers continue to retire, it is only getting worse.

What's more is that Canadians and those in other developed countries are living longer than ever before. This creates a problem for both life insurers and policyholders. The policyholder that lives longer than expected will find themselves having to pay out more in total number of premiums than expected. Clearly no one wants to die early, but you do want your premiums to accurately reflect the actual value of your policy.

Believe it or not, insurance companies are also struggling with increased life expectancies. You are probably wondering why insurance companies would suffer from people living longer and thus paying more out in premiums. The answer requires knowledge of the industry. Canadians living longer might seem like a good thing for insurance companies, as they are able to collect more in premiums, but the truth is that these same insurance companies have two main sources of revenue: policies *and* annuities. Because insurance companies are so heavily invested in annuities, which continue to pay guaranteed payouts over the course of a recipient's life, longer lifespans are cutting into insurers' bottom line significantly!

- Good point
- on annuities - especially if they are 10-15 years old already

SPILLING THE BEANS

The Changing Landscape of the Life Insurance Market

EVER SINCE THE events of September 11, 2001, the life insurance markets have never been the same. The life insurance industry had never before seen so many claims caused by one black-swan event. With the collapse of the World Trade Center towers, insurance companies saw a deluge of simultaneous premature payouts due to the number of wealth individuals lost in the attacks. This put a strain on the industry, but more importantly, completely changed the way insurance companies calculate risk. The unthinkable turned out to be not all that unthinkable and, indeed, quite possible.

This risk is now being factored into the price and availability of policies, and the underwriting process has become far more difficult. The life insurance industry has become especially adverse to the risk of larger policies, which place them at the greatest exposure. A large policy before 9/11 was in the area of $130 million. After the events of September 11, 2001, the average larger-sized policy was only about $20 million to $30 million, and it has taken the industry until now, over a decade, to finally return to pre-9/11 policies. But make no mistake: a similar event would again take larger policies off the market, perhaps forever this time. Such an event will happen; it is only a matter of time.

In fact, it already has: the 2008 market meltdown and the ensuing financial crisis. Though largely framed as a housing and subprime mortgage crisis in the United States, in reality, the financial meltdown cut across all sectors of the economy. The major insurance companies that dominate the market for large-policy life insurance in Canada experienced a plunge in stock value of more than 50 percent, severe equity loss, and a strain on their capital reserves. This has worried regulators in Ottawa who fear the collapse of an overextended life insurance industry, and the ongoing fallout has precipitated current and planned changes in life insurance industry regulations.

While these changes may or may not be good for the industry, they are definitely bad for individual consumers. The changes to regulation have resulted in the removal and gutting of tax-advantaged products, which provide the best strategic and financial returns to our clients. It has further driven down the availability of larger plans and limited the amount of coverage you can get.

Though the industry has returned to issuing larger policies again, they are now far more difficult to attain. Life insurance companies now contract with an average of six to eight reinsurance companies in order to diffuse their exposure to risk. These reinsurance companies also contract with multiple retrocessionaires (that re-insure the re-insurers!) to further spread out their exposure. This diffusion of risk is, on its face, a good thing. The problem, particularly for the life-insurance applicant, is that all of these reinsurance companies and retrocessionaires place their own demands upon the underwriting process (the process under which you apply for insurance and are vetted by these companies) and have made attaining larger-policy life insurance both arduous and uncertain. More and more applicants are being denied the full coverage they need.

This sharing of risk is good for the Canadian life insurance companies when it comes to risk mitigation, but they have lost control of the underwriting process to a large extent. These reinsurance and retrocessionaires, many of whom are offshore, have a stake in and can make further demands upon the applicant, which they have been doing by and large. Applicants can now expect to be asked for excessive information about their personal and business lives. They can also expect to face more medical requirements. They may even be subjected to very intrusive requests for information and demands. If you don't play ball, you don't get life insurance. It is a really unfortunate situation and, I won't lie to you, quite unpleasant.

At Ocean West Financial Group, we do everything we can to make the process as efficient and comfortable for the clients as possible while still maximizing their chance at getting the coverage they need. We have built a rapport with many life insurance companies and reinsurers, both in

Canada and abroad, so that we can better understand their processes and priorities. We want to help our clients put their best foot forward so that they can be insurable as early as possible in order to get through the process successfully. We also try to make the process less unpleasant by doing most of the arrangements. We send town cars to bring the client to and from appointments so they can work while they are in transit, for example.

In the world of life insurance, underwriters determine your health and risks in order to see if you qualify for coverage. This is not—unfortunately—a cut and dry process. These so-called underwriters work not for you, but for their individual companies—so guess whose interests they have in mind? And don't forget, you're not just dealing with the insurance companies' underwriters. The reinsurers and retrocessionaires all have their own underwriters. These secondary underwriters go back over the insurance company's underwriters, dig deeper, and usually come back with more questions and demands. Because all of these underwriters work for different companies with different risk exposure, they therefore place different demands upon the applicant. The whole thing has become a mess and exceedingly difficult to navigate on your own. Your financial advisors won't be much help with the underwriting process—you need someone with intimate knowledge of the industry, a true insurance specialist like our team at Ocean West Financial Group.

SPILLING THE BEANS

There are strict guidelines by which underwriters are supposed to assess your application for insurance, but they necessarily exercise a high degree of discretion in grey areas, of which there are many. This may sound fine, but the process is fraught with loopholes, potential mistakes and misunderstandings, and the possibility of plain, bad decisions being made by the underwriters on the insurance company's behalf. Underwriters don't like grey areas; their business is risk management, and so they err on the side of caution. In many cases, underwriters pass on individuals who would actually make wonderful clients.

The bottom line is this: Canadian life insurance companies have lost control over the underwriting process, and there are now layers upon layers of factors and new complexities in the underwriting process. The strategic sophistication an advanced insurance specialist provides is now a necessity for life insurance applicants. The more complex your application (read: the larger the policy), the more this is true. Larger-policy life insurance is a relatively small market, and there are few specialists that have the level of understanding and expertise needed to see you through the process successfully as we do at Ocean West Financial Group. We are experts at working on cases in the $10 million to over $100 million range. Simply put: few people work with policies of this size and complexity.

G. KIM HINKSON

Your Options Are Being Regulated Away

FURTHERMORE, UNDERWRITERS AND the insurance companies themselves are facing major changes to regulation. They are operating in a changing, unsure environment, and it has them scared—oftentimes they are passing on individuals who really should be granted coverage. While changing demographics are increasing the demand for life insurance, current and proposed regulation changes are poised to severely affect the supply side of the equation. Some of the best products—those with a significant tax-advantaged investment component—are being pulled off the market. This is something I warn my clients about every day. Certain products are literally under attack from government regulators, and their time is short.

Earlier we discussed utilizing strategies that take advantage of the tax efficiencies of exempt policies that can save you enough in taxes through the deduction of the loan interest to offset the cost of your premiums, effectively making your insurance policy of zero net cost for most individuals. These tax savings are dependent upon the exempt status, and certain exempt policies are being overhauled and taken off the market.

So what dictates whether a policy is exempt or not?

The Income Tax Act outlines the rules for determining if a policy is eligible for exemption. The Act contains a section on the Exempt Policy Test, which is designed for this very purpose: to differentiate life insurance policies that are investment oriented from those that are designed for protection, the latter of which is the traditional role of insurance. The Act is intended to prevent "unfair" tax advantages associated with exempt insurance policies being used as an investment-account tax shelter—which, for those of us working in estate preservation, limits the options available to consumers. The government is squashing strategies that are too good to be true—namely, those policies that guaranteed an unrealistic return. The government only wants to allow policies that can stand on their own. Basically, they are allowing for market risk.

Though the government has been clear that there will be changes, they clearly support some level of tax sheltering based on the fact that they are grandfathering in older plans and still allowing some tax-advantaged life insurance options, though far fewer and only at what amounts to a greater cost.

This makes total sense—the Act wants to avoid exploitation of the rules and avoid giving unfair tax advantages for policies that are really just investment vehicles under the guise of insurance protection in order to dodge taxes. However, the fact is that many entrepreneurs legitimately do need these very large policies as *protection* for their businesses, and there is no reason that the government should penalize them

G. KIM HINKSON

[handwritten margin note: As a Canadian citizen you have a fiduciary responsibility to pay as little tax as possible]

for doing so. Who is to say that the protection is ancillary to the tax advantages? Entrepreneurs should get the same tax breaks as anyone else, and there is no reason you should not take advantage of the deductions available to you. Furthermore, for high-net-worth individuals, there is often no way for them to obtain affordable succession planning and estate preservation without these larger policies because they are worth so much to their companies and in net assets. Many of our clients are being, in a way, "priced out of the market" *because* of their wealth. The more you are worth, the less likely you will be able to get the full coverage that you need, and, again, it is only going to get worse.

[handwritten margin note: good point]

That's because, very soon, these tax advantages and the benefits of being fully covered without gaps of exposure may not be available to you any longer *at any price*. If you want your policy to be grandfathered in under the current rules, you need to have your policy in place before the changes come into effect. The proposed changes that affect the exempt ceiling just came out in September and will kick in as soon as 2016.

Wholesale reform of life-insurance strategies is unlikely, but experts agree that changes will decrease your options and increase the net cost of life insurance. While we can't yet know exactly what the proposed changes to exempt policy regulation will look like in their final legal form, experts note that changes are almost certain to include a reduction in the maximum premium and policy size (currently at $130 million) and in the maximum cash value accumulations allowed. In other words, you will pay more taxes on your policy, which will have a decreased level of tax-deferred growth, and you might have your access to full coverage limited. We know this because that is the whole point of the changes: to reduce the tax advantages available to high-net-worth individuals, who would otherwise be making use of these benefits by reinvesting in their businesses.

Because the tax advantages associated with exempt life-insurance policies are so significant, it is absolutely imperative that you maintain exempt status in the face of the government's attempts to reduce the tax sheltering opportunity. You need someone who both truly understands the current system as well as the proposed and likely changes.

Above all, for those entrepreneurs who have needs now that can be best met by life insurance or aren't sure they are in the right product and need to revisit life-insurance options, I encourage you to act now. Anyone with a policy in place between now and 2016 should expect grandfathering. If you don't go into an exempt policy until after 2016, you will face reduced benefits to tax sheltering due to changes to the MTAR rule. MTAR stands for the Maximum Tax Actuarial Reserve, which sets the limit for how much you can accumulate in investments within your life insurance policy. This is calculated as a ratio between the portion of the premium covering the cost of insuring your life and the investment component of the policy. Currently this ratio is about 1:3 to 1:4, but will go down further in 2016. This lowers the ceiling for tax-sheltered investment potential.

There will be a huge financial benefit to those individuals and businesses that hold grandfathered higher-ceiling tax-exempt policies, and the disparity will place businesses and entrepreneurs on uneven, unfair terrain. This is unfortunate and clearly unfair, but while you cannot change the well-intentioned but misguided legislation, you can move to position yourself for the long term before the changes take place.

Vanishing Guarantees

SOME REGULATIONS ARE actually well-intentioned. The regulators governing the banking and insurance industries have done a good job of protecting us in the past—Canada was the most unscathed country in the industrialized world during the 2008 financial crisis because of effective regulation. And the truth is that the larger-policy life insurance industry as it is structured now is quite unsustainable and, without changes, will struggle financially. This is why we know there will be changes: because the model no longer works in the current economic climate. The biggest problem facing the industry right now is one of its own creation: guarantees, which it can no longer continue to promise and offer. The industry can simply not continue to be profitable if it continues to promise guarantees to deliver specific benefits to the policyholder.

This is unfortunate for future applicants because these guarantees are highly valuable, and once they are gone, you will be at a disadvantage. Those who hold grandfathered plans with guarantees will be in quite an elite and advantaged club! There is a real and legitimate concern about overregulation and the amount of grief it could cause the life insurance industry and consumers worldwide. The fact is that some of these products are simply too good to be true, and they are going to have to go away eventually. If you want to get in on them before they vanish, you have a short window to do so.

So what happened to guarantees to make them so unsustainable? First, let me explain the different types of life insurance plans that are currently available.

What many people think of when they think of traditional life insurance is what the industry calls "term life insurance." This is where the policyholder pays regular premiums for what is usually a fixed benefit. These benefits only last for a specified amount of time, after which premiums and benefits cease to exist. This is traditional insurance and is really only good for risk management and to provide replacement income to the family of the deceased. If the term is not sufficient to cover the entirety of your possible lifespan, then these products are no good for succession planning and estate preservation.

Our advanced insurance strategies utilize permanent life-insurance plans because you obviously want to be sure that your benefits pay out upon your passing, and because these policies are structured to have an investment component. The most typical types are "whole life" insurance (permanent coverage until death that can have a tax-sheltered investment component), "term to 100" (which is term, but the term period of a hundred years is longer than you are likely to live, making it essentially a permanent product), and "universal life" (another permanent policy that allows for investments to be placed back into the policy without being taxed).

Generally speaking, we work with permanent policies like "universal," "whole life," and "term to 100." All of these policies are useful to us only because they can be linked to an investment account, allowing us creative ways of utilizing them to your advantage, and because they are permanent and they can provide guaranteed benefits.

So those are the main tools we work with, and every day, we use them to benefit our clients. The only problem with these tools is that they are now disappearing because of vanishing guarantees. In the last few decades, we saw an increase in the number of life insurance policies that were being backed by variable-rate annuities. These policies tied the benefit payouts to market returns while also continuing to promise policyholders a minimum guaranteed income. This worked great in a high-interest-rate environment, but now that we are stuck in a low-interest-rate quagmire, as explained earlier, the guarantees have become unserviceable.

The other thing affecting insurance companies' ability to offer guarantees is government regulation. Insurance companies are compelled by regulation to retain a certain percentage of capital in a reserve account for each guarantee.

Low interest rates further compound this because the reserve amount is inversely related to the returns/interest rate. This means that in the current environment, insurance

G. KIM HINKSON

companies must now hold more capital without being able to reinvest it, which makes their returns even lower. It is a vicious cycle that is making it impossible for insurance companies to offer the same levels of guarantees that they did only a decade or two ago. This regulation, which is in response to the excesses in the financial industry, with which these investment-oriented life insurance policies are closely tied, is well intentioned but it forces insurance companies into an expensive way of doing business. Forcing companies to set aside capital in a reserve account lowers the amount that they have to reinvest in their businesses. It puts the company into a bad financial situation by arbitrarily limiting a company's economic capital.

The insurance industry is adjusting, but they are doing so by slashing guarantees.

The cost of offering guarantees on today's products is very expensive for life insurance companies and, in my expert opinion, unsustainable. Although the insurance companies have built the cost guarantees into the product, changes in interest rates and the amount of "reserves" or capital these companies are required to set aside by the government have made them unworkable for insurance companies to offer. Some products have been pulled from the market in the last few months, and many other products featuring guarantees have been revamped, re-priced, or completely removed from the market. Often the whole product itself will be removed because it can't be sustained without the guarantees—without the guarantee, they are worthless anyway.

So you can see that many of these permanent life-insurance policies and products, and especially those with an investment component, are under attack from both the government and the very industry that has been offering them. They may not entirely go away, but they will certainly be nerfed. This is the primary manifestation of the changing landscape of the market and the restructuring of the industry from the inside and out.

This is what we mean by scarcity. If the life insurance industry continues on this course, it will have to remove all guarantees and other investment products, not just because the government is making them, but simply as a matter of self-preservation. Even "term to 100," the simplest form of investment-oriented life insurance that underpins the other types of insurance we use, may soon go away. If the industry cannot sustain this type of product, it will utterly change the landscape of the life insurance industry in Canada, at least for new applicants who do not have grandfathered policies in place. The industry will be literally unrecognizable.

Understand that these changes are already underway and that more dramatic changes are on the way. **The opportunity to buy and use certain guaranteed products for lifelong succession planning is coming to an end.** Unless you are grandfathered in soon, you will lose the opportunity to lock in these plans as well as the substantial financial and security benefits that come with them. Entrepreneurs can no longer afford to wait based on these facts alone. Between the changes to the Tax Exempt Test and vanishing guarantees, you may not have the opportunities tomorrow that you have at your disposal today. Putting the right policy in place now is the best thing you can do to address your exposures while taking advantage of the best options available to you. Delay your decision and you will lose access to what are perhaps the most significant, cost-effective tools available to you for succession planning, estate preservation, and tax-advantaged investing for large investment accounts. You don't have a lot of options with the latter—it's not like you can park $100 million in an RRSP!

SPILLING THE BEANS

Life Can Happen Overnight—
Will You Be Insurable Tomorrow?

SO WE KNOW that, generally speaking, access to life insurance is tightening, but how does this affect *your* access to life insurance?

Successful entrepreneurs are savvy people, and so you probably understand that life-insurance options available to you will decline as you age. The nature of insurance makes it unlikely for an underwriter to give the same policy to someone who is seventy years old as they would offer someone who is fifty. This, of course, makes intuitive sense: the younger you are, the less of a risk you are to the insurance company and the longer they are likely to extract premiums from you. This results in lower premiums and a higher overall insurability for the young that diminishes with age.

What you may fail to realize, though, is that you can become less insurable—even uninsurable—overnight. While we age in a uniform manner, we experience health problems and diagnoses in an unpredictable way. The fact is that a single diagnosis, lab result, or medical event, no matter how minor, can affect *your* access to life insurance. So while you may understand that you cannot afford to put off getting life insurance until you are seventy, you need to realize that it is not something you can delay *at all*. When you are worth as much as our clients are, there is just no room for this kind of exposure—the stakes are too high.

We get it: you're a busy business professional with a lot—*a whole lot*—on your plate. And you may think you can delay action a few years because you will be basically the same age, basically still in the same age group. But this is not the Nielsen demographics—this is the real world, where a single event can change everything when it comes to the underwriting process.

Why the Underwriting Process Matters

SO FAR WE have looked at the ways in which the life insurance industry is changing and taking products off the market wholesale. But there is more to the story: due to the extreme tightening of the market, individual applicants are finding themselves excluded from full coverage and even those products still currently available. In the current climate, small business owners over the age of forty who have a combined net worth in excess of $15 million can expect a challenge obtaining a standard offer that covers their entire exposure—despite having good health.

Be forewarned: there is a radical difference between the health assessment you receive from your own doctor and the one you will receive from life insurance companies—the latter are not simply performing clinical diagnoses. You probably have a longstanding relationship with your family doctor, and they likely have a deep and comprehensive understanding of your lifestyle and health risks. Patients develop a rapport and personal relationship with their doctors, which allows such healthcare providers to give you a more accurate, albeit less objective, professional assessment of your health than anything you are going to experience with an insurance company underwriter.

What you need to understand first and foremost is that life insurance company underwriters are assessing you not for health risks as a doctor would, but for the risk and exposure you present to their company and its shareholders. Therefore, their assessment is cold, clinical, and thorough in delving into areas not relevant to your immediate health—these underwriters leave no stone unturned. It may actually be a more objective assessment than what a healthcare provider would perform, but it is often less accurate. Underwriters tend to look for certain metrics, and failing to meet a single benchmark can derail your entire application for coverage. Often, the metric that results in your denial, while perhaps a risk when taken alone, poses no real risk when considered in the context of your overall health. I see this happen all of the time. The life insurance company doesn't care, because in the current economic climate, they can't even risk the possibility of risk.

Take, for example, one of my clients whom we will call John. He was a relatively young man who had turned his small business into a burgeoning national company. We began working with him by utilizing The Smart Strategies Program®, the process by which we work with clients to determine and implement the best custom-tailored strategies for their situation and needs. (Skip to the end of the book for more on this process.)

We walked him through the Fact Finding process to determine his situation and then, during the "Vision Conversation" and "Strategy Innovator" steps (in which we bring back facts to his team and together build a case around them), we determined that his life insurance needs amounted to $100 million. This is close to the maximum amount you can obtain in Canada. Our financial analysis of his situation also identified a need to fully insure his company's key people, including the CFO and eight of the minority shareholders. We drafted ten applications for insurance in all. For everyone but the primary insured policy holder/majority shareholder, the medical portion of the application was a simple questionnaire and minimal medical testing that could be done from home or office.

The primary, however, needed to undergo testing at a private healthcare facility chosen by the underwriters (we prefer to use our own medical network of doctors we can trust) in order to take an electrocardiogram (ECG) test on a specialized treadmill. They wanted to be sure he had no heart problems. The test went fine and he returned to work. We had the doctor send the results over to the insurance companies for their initial review. The insurance company flags any oddities before they, in turn, send the files off to the reinsurers, usually five companies, who do the same. He had to go through more than one ECG, two hours of testing and questionnaires, blood and urine analysis, and more. All of this, as you can imagine, was and is highly intrusive.

We consider medical testing one of the most intrusive and uncomfortable parts of the application process. At

[Margin note: A bit too much selling]

Ocean West Financial Group, we understand the anguish of having to take precious time away from work and family to deal with doctors and nurses. This is why we streamline the process to make it as comfortable and efficient as possible. With our top-tier clients, we offer a town car pickup and drop-off to and from a private healthcare facility so that they can work while they are in transit. This facility is expensive, but we want our clients in the hands of the best medical practitioners—ones we can trust not to undermine the underwriting process unnecessarily. Someone from our office—either me or my assistant—will meet the clients at the end of their medical appointment to make sure everything went well and to inform them of what needs to be done next.

At the point of John's "surprise" ECG, we had already obtained reports from his doctors on behalf of the insurance company so that he would not have to waste time figuring out and filing them himself. This way the underwriters had everything they needed right away. This is just one more example of how we streamline the process and involve you, the client, as little as is necessary in such mundane minutia. We did this for John and within days we received a phone call from the lead underwriter indicating that there was a potential concern with a recent neurological assessment and a lymph node gland. They requested that we obtain additional information from the client's family doctor.

SPILLING THE BEANS

When we consulted John, he informed us that, according to him, the neurological assessment was simply a misunderstanding: during a recent annual medical physical for executives, he had asked the doctor if there was anything unusual about not remembering people's names. He had noticed that he had had trouble recalling the names of business associates recently. The doctor said it sounded like no big deal, and he was probably just hyper-focusing on what are normal faults in human memory, but just to be safe, she referred him to a neurologist. The neurologist's assessment was that everything was fine, but he suggested a follow-up in a few months as a standard precautionary measure—there were no signs of Alzheimer's or any other serious ailment. He assured the client it was nothing to be worried about.

Well, the underwriters at the reinsurance companies had a different take on the situation. They demanded a further neurological assessment, this time using a particular, designed test they employed.

And the lymph node? They demanded a biopsy or prophylactic removal of the lymph node. We made contact once again with the client. We also contacted his executive assistant and the CFO, who had been very involved from the outset, both of them assisting us in gathering the financial information required for underwriting. We were overseeing the situation, which is one of our core strengths: coaching and quarterbacking the situation strategically. Working with his team and their advisors, we found a way to expedite both the biopsy appointment and the requested appointment with a trusted neurologist in our business network. We trusted this person to be able to accurately interpret the results from the required test.

The results: the lymph node biopsy showed no change in the past year, which was both great financial and personal news for the client. The neurologist administered the required test, which had five parts. The client received a normal grade in three out of the five, but failed two—he was given an overall "normal" grade.

Normal. That's what you want to hear, right?

Not according to the insurance company underwriters! The reinsurers were still not satisfied with the fact that the biopsy showed nothing had changed. This was partly due to the high level of insurance we were applying for. With these big policies, underwriters try to avoid even the potential for risk or exposure. They don't want uncertainty. His results were in a grey area—possibly concerning, but probably not. Due to this uncertainty, they did not know how to measure his risk. Operating in a grey area like this, underwriters are forced to use their own discretion, which they do not want to do on a larger policy. It is easier to just deny or limit coverage.

In this client's case, they were only willing to go forward if he had the lymph node removed prophylactically! His doctor kept insisting there was no change to his health and that the lymph node did not need to be removed, but the insurers demanded it. This is completely intrusive, but in cases like this, the underwriters can really have you against a wall. Because this is so intrusive and the client did not want to have unnecessary surgery at the insurance company's behest; we are working with the underwriters to reach a mutually amicable agreement.

The takeaway here is how intrusive and high-stakes the process is. It highlights how much control the insurance companies have over you during the underwriting process. Right now, we have the process postponed for six months, which is not ideal because any further changes to John's health can derail the process totally, but we are working to meet his needs. In the end, I don't know who will win out, John and the other clients and their doctors … or the underwriters, but we are working with an underwriting specialist helping us to re-approach the situation.

We are hoping for the best results, but the delay is not ideal. And here is why: while all of this was happening, two of the minority shareholders, who had already cleared the medical portion of the application, were deemed to have substantial medical issues—one had had a minor skin cancer removed and a weight issue. These are not significant medical issues, but the insurance underwriters flagged them as risky anyway. Also, the CFO, with whom we had developed a good relationship, had gone to see his doctor due to unusual symptoms of stomach irritation—upon further testing, he was diagnosed with a rare form of intestinal cancer. We were saddened and floored.

All of this came after the CFO had completed the insurance application and medical exams and had received a standard offer—we just hadn't delivered the policy. But what happened was, the CFO got the bad news and we had the fiduciary responsibility to report changes in health to the insurance company. The initial offer was now terminated.

We literally had the policy ready to deliver to him for signing and now it was gone in a flash, just like that. I am telling you: do not delay on anything or this is what can happen. If this had happened two weeks later, he would have been fully insured.

The bottom line: we were not able to insure the CFO, but were able to insure the primary policyholder and all eight minority shareholders for a combined total of only $57 million. That is $25 million for the primary policyholder that covers the buy–sell agreement. Clearly, this falls far short of the $100 million we had applied for and that the client truly needed, and the CFO represents serious exposure to everyone involved if he passes away and a buy–sell agreement triggers. The policy is far better than nothing, and the best he could have hoped for given the circumstances, but clearly it leaves gaps of exposure in his coverage.

This was something of a workaround, and while not ideal, is a good step in the right direction considering the circumstances we encountered while trying to get John and his company through the underwriting process. Let this be a cautionary tale. We put the best underwriting specialist in Canada on John's case; without our network of specialists and our unique expertise, he might have been denied coverage completely. This just goes to show that you really need someone with a comprehensive knowledge of the industry like we have at Ocean West—the market is complex and unintuitive, and you really need someone on your side who has the experience to ensure that you don't get denied the coverage you deserve.

Luckily, John already had a term life insurance policy with another Canadian insurance company, which we recommended converting to permanent insurance in order to further close exposure gaps. All of the reinsurance companies postponed any decision on his application for six months—at this time, he, the primary, will have to again undergo more medical testing. We are still working with him on the process, trying to get his full application approved. We have a working relationship with an underwriting consultant who has strong relationships with the reinsurance community, and we are working with them to help John get the positive outcome he needs. We are confident we can continue to help John but we cannot be certain of the outcome.

Again, the thing to understand about the underwriting process is that the underwriters are not working for you—they are working for the (many) insurance companies involved, whose best interests they have in mind, not yours. With so much money on the line, underwriters err on the side of caution when making discretionary decisions. The lesson is this: you had better have a damn good advanced insurance advisor on your side working your application, making your case, and advocating for your interests. You want someone who knows how to manage the logistics of the underwriting process and the complexities involved in your application. The application is replete with pitfalls, as is your personal history. You need to be able to not only put your best foot forward in your application, but you also need to do so in the right way to avoid unnecessarily or unduly spooking the underwriters. Otherwise, you are going to find that your application ends up as tinder in someone's fireplace.

We love John—he's one of our favorite clients, but let him be a cautionary tale: avoid the headaches and risks he has had to deal with. Find a knowledgeable advanced insurance specialist and get the process started—the right way—without delay. Due to the limited size of the market, as very few individuals qualify for these larger policies, there are few true specialists in these advanced insurance strategies. We advise you not to take chances with someone who does not know the lay of the land. You will be hard-pressed to find a company with more experience in the larger-policy life insurance than the specialists at Ocean West Financial Group. We know we sound like we are marketing—and we are—but we have the experience and the expertise to back it up.

G. KIM HINKSON

What We Can Do for You

BY THIS POINT, I hope I have imparted upon you the need you have for a true expert in our advanced insurance strategies. Make no mistake: I am a businessperson and I am trying to sell you our services. I am not in the business of marketing; I am in the business of providing strategic answers to your succession planning and estate preservation by utilizing the best life-insurance-as-investment-planning options available to you. Ocean West Financial Group is here to help you strategize and implement a comprehensive, affordable, effective, no-gaps-allowed solution to the exposure problems you may not even know you had.

Our unique value and ability as a company is this: we have identified and established a collection of meaningful relationships with other unique individuals and companies that are major players and experts in the life insurance industry. These companies have developed their own niche products that can work together synergistically if they are implanted well. We act as a conduit and navigator, helping facilitate the process by bringing you, the client, together with the purveyors of the best life insurance products out there, their advisors, our team of specialists, and your own team of advisors, specialists, and partners.

We want to stress that we do not take the place of your advisors. We work with them. Your financial advisors, medical professionals, tax specialists, and business partners must all be keyed in and involved in the process. It is absolutely critical that everyone involved in the process is on the same page. Do key in any business partners about the process and make sure that they are all on the same page and embracing the process—this will lead to the greatest efficiency and efficacy. As we have said, ideally all of your business partners will be fully insured along with you so that everyone in your business (and their families) are protected by fully funded buy–sell agreements. Shareholders in your company may need to be insured, also.

It is also extremely important to be strategic about working with your medical providers. You may trust your doctors with your health, but would you trust them with your succession plan and the preservation of your estate? Because that is exactly what you are doing when you allow them to meddle with the underwriting process without being aware of the ramifications of their actions. At Ocean West Financial Group, we work carefully with the client to make sure that they are not seeking medical aid unless necessary until the underwriting process is over. We also plug you in with our own team of medical experts, who are fully briefed in the underwriting process and can be trusted to keep not only your health in mind but also your financial situation and insurance needs.

We want to be clear: we are not urging you to avoid needed medical attention. We are, however, very much urging you to be mindful of what tests you undergo during the underwriting process and not to dally—you need to get through the process as quickly as possible and get your policy in place. During this process, you want to avoid making unnecessary trips to the doctor and avoid taking unneeded medical tests. If you can put off a test until after the process is over, it might behoove you to do so. You want to be careful with and mind your health and your business interests.

So as you can see, there are many players in the process with their own needs, concerns, responsibilities, and interests. It isn't just you we work with. We work with your partners, your specialists, your advisors. We work with your family. We work with underwriters from the insurance companies, the reinsurance companies, and their retrocessionaires. We work with the companies and institutions that are the purveyors of the financial products and plans that we work with. With so many players, there is just too much risk of mistake and misstep. There is no way you will be able to navigate the process as efficiently and effectively as you would with a true expert in the industry—there are just too many players and factors involved and the stakes are too high.

That's where Ocean West Financial Group comes in. Our core strength as a company is in managing, strategizing, and quarterbacking your and our entire team through the process of implementing the best life-insurance strategy possible.

Our process is successful because it is designed to be both effective and efficient. It is designed around an understanding of your busy schedule as a highly active and busy entrepreneur and business owner. Out of respect for and an understanding of our clients' busy schedules, we do not involve them any more than is necessary. We allow for efficient use of advisors, and we pick up the fees of advisors as it relates to your life insurance and succession planning so that you don't have to deal with paying contractors. We will clearly explain to you and your advisors exactly what to do, file, write, say, etc. And we will work with you through the entire process—forever. We do annual reviews and stay in touch to make sure everything stays in order. This is a lifelong relationship process, though we keep it minimally involved.

We stay in touch and continue to coach and offer whatever you need when it comes to succession planning. Absolutely whatever is required. We are there to help. We provide added value by accessing our extended resources and relationships in niche areas such as business mentors, coaches, medical experts, and more so we can eliminate problems and help our clients become more successful in their businesses. Whatever you need. We don't just coach—because you don't need another advisor—we quarterback, we strategize, we implement. That's where our core value lies.

The Smart Strategies Program®

YOU MAY NOW be asking yourself, how, *specifically*, do we do all of this?

Earlier, I have talked extensively about our advanced insurance strategies. The best strategy varies too much from client to client to be able to give you relevant advice to your unique situation here. What I can share with you is our unique trademarked process that we call The Smart Strategies Program®. I won't bore you with too many of the details of the program, because without a specialist to assess your unique situation and prepare and walk you through the underwriting process, The Smart Strategies Program® will not do you any good. These are not our advanced insurance strategies per se—it is the process by which we identify and implement the best strategies for you.

The seven steps of The Smart Strategies Program® in a nutshell:

1. The Vision Conversation

Every program we develop is custom designed to meet the unique needs of each client, taking into consideration their business and personal goals, family situation, estate plan, core values, and of course, the facts as they relate to corporate and personal financials.

2. The Strategy Innovator

Our advanced insurance specialists use the Fact Finder information to identify the most effective financial strategy tailored to each client's unique situation and needs.

3. The Advisor Consultation

We work hand-in-hand with accounting and legal experts to provide added value and the best possible advice as part of a comprehensive financial strategy.

4. The Client Commitment

We provide the necessary details to understand and maximize The Smart Strategies Program®.

5. The Underwriting Process

We understand the demands on our client's day-to-day schedules and will facilitate a convenient and professional, executive-level service to ensure you obtain the best offer to maximize the benefits of The Smart Strategies Program®.

6. The Implementation Process

We operate on the premise that we only succeed when our clients succeed, and provide detailed information for sound documentation.

7. *The Annual Review Package*

A guaranteed annual package will detail Smart Strategies results, and as business situations and personal circumstances change, we're right there to make necessary adjustments to ensure your financial strategy is on track.

So that is the process by which we navigate you through the world of large-policy life insurance and succession planning. At times, it becomes necessary to take a short diversion from The Smart Strategies Program® when something comes up that could impede the success of your application. We remain flexible and attentive to your needs—there's no room for rigidity in this business!

That's because these kinds of diversions are, unfortunately, common due to the difficult nature of the underwriting process. And I will be honest: until your policy is in place, nothing is guaranteed. Sometimes significant roadblocks, such as a major medical or partnership issue, can derail the process. In these cases we may be able to achieve only limited success until there is a resolution, as in the case of John and his co-applicants. Due to the complexity of the process and market, these circumstances are practically inevitable.

This is, however, exactly why you need us on your side. Putting in an application for life insurance is not that complicated. But getting the best coverage is. It is in these instances when our clients truly reap the benefits of our expertise and our collection of unique relationships with specialists and insurers. Usually we can solve the problem in short order and get back on track with The Smart Strategies Program®! Other times, significant roadblocks require a complete change of strategy. Whatever the case, we urge you to realize that you do not have to, and should not, make this journey alone.

Remember, The Smart Strategies Program® is the process for identifying the best strategy, not a custom-tailored strategy on its own. The right strategy for your situation is unique to you, and we urge you to contact us to continue the conversation. Visit our website at www.oceanwestfg.com to read more about our company and who we are, what we stand for and do, how we work, and what we can do for you.

We hope this book has really Spilled the Beans on the life insurance industry for you and opened your eyes to your own potential exposure. But nothing can substitute for the individual in-person attention we can offer our clients. If you are a high-net-worth individual and/or own your own company and you lack comprehensive life insurance and a solid succession plan, or if you are unsure if your current plans and policies are sufficient to keep you fully covered, we invite you to please reach out to us.

You can also reach us by phone at 604-662-3150 or call us toll free at 1-888-287-1111.

My personal email is kim.hinkson@oceanwestfg.com. You can read my blog and more about our company at our website, which is, again, www.oceanwestfg.com.

Advanced insurance specialty

AMCAR

Mark to Market Rules could include
Life insurance (Page 14
    underwriting good story
Create Urgency
Genetics, Nano Tech, DNA Profile
Private medical companies etc

Reinsurance good comment
oligopoly

grandfathers - 10.5 did not
Priced out of Market due to
Wealth

Reasoning is a problem
New Accounting Rules don't work
for insurance companies

Lee Baral insurance products
older Market

Shareholder Risk and 2 mutual
companies left —